To my son, Steven

# Steven and the Green Turtle

## by William J. Cromie
### Pictures by Tom Eaton

SCHOLASTIC BOOK SERVICES
NEW YORK · TORONTO · LONDON · AUCKLAND · SYDNEY · TOKYO

ISBN 0-590-30904-8

Text copyright © 1970 by William J. Cromie. Pictures copyright © 1970 by Tom Eaton. All rights reserved. This edition is published by Scholastic Book Services, a division of Scholastic Magazines, Inc., 50 West 44th Street, New York, New York 10036, by arrangement with Harper & Row Publishers, Inc.

12 11 10 9 8 7 6 5 4 3 2 1          11          9/7  0  1  2  3  4/8

# Steven and the Green Turtle

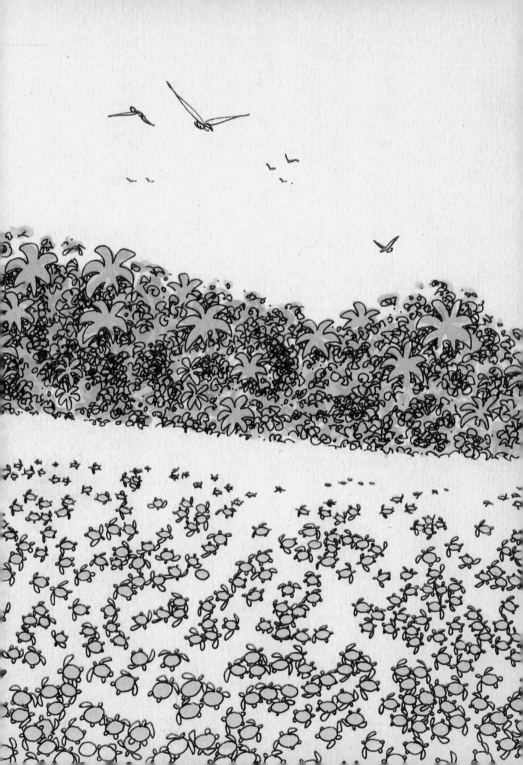

# PART I

It was the strangest thing
Steven had ever seen.
There were hundreds of baby turtles
on the beach.

Steven lived in Costa Rica.

He often saw big adult turtles.

But he had never seen baby turtles.

U.S.A.

MEXICO

BRITISH
HONDURAS

HONDURAS

GUATEMALA

**NICKY'S ROUTE**
**STEVEN'S VILLAGE**

EL SALVADOR

NICARAGUA

**COSTA RICA**

PANAMA

Crabs were coming out of holes.

They chased the little turtles.

One crab grabbed a turtle

with its sharp claws.

The crab began to drag the turtle

toward its hole.

Steven caught the turtle.

He tried to pull it free.

The crab held on.

Then Steven hit the crab

against a log.

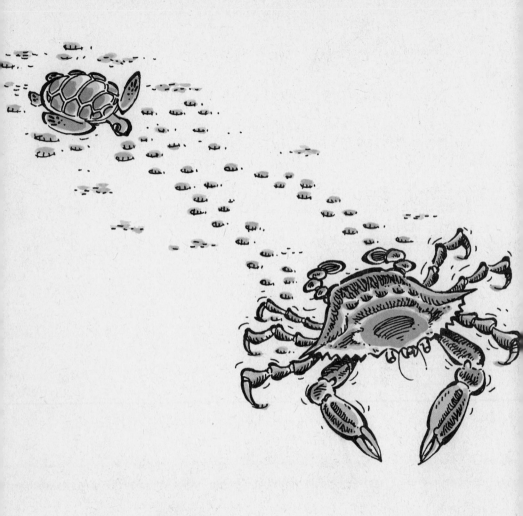

That did it!

The crab let go and ran away.

The baby turtle was free.

The turtle had flippers.

Its back flippers were round

like Ping-Pong paddles.

Its front flippers looked

like little wings.

They had nicks in their edges.

Steven had never seen a turtle

with nicks in its flippers.

"I think I'll call you Nicky,"

Steven said. "You are nice.

Maybe I will keep you for a pet."

Then he changed his mind.

"I will find a turtle

that was not born with nicks."

He looked around for a better turtle.

Suddenly Steven heard a bark.

He saw a dog following the turtles.

The dog ate one of them.

Then Steven saw the dog near Nicky.

"Get away from that turtle!"

Steven yelled.

He chased the dog away.

Steven watched Nicky

going toward the ocean.

The little turtle was

slow and clumsy.

A bird flew at Nicky.

Steven ran to help the turtle.

The bird's beak closed over Nicky.

The bird started to fly away.

Steven put Nicky

in a pail of seawater.

He went to the river with a net.

He caught some tiny shrimp.

He gave them to Nicky.

The turtle ate them.

Nicky grew very fast.

Soon thè turtle was too big

for the pail.

Steven's father built

a big wooden tank for Nicky.

The turtle kept growing.

When Nicky was one year old,

Steven needed two hands

to pick the turtle up.

No tank was big enough

to hold Nicky.

Steven's father built a pen

in the sea.

The new pen was big enough

for the turtle.

It was big enough

to hold Steven too.

Every day he swam with his pet.

They played together for hours.

Steven taught Nicky to play tag.

He touched the turtle on the head.

Then he swam away quickly.

The turtle followed Steven.

It touched him with its beak.

Because he had Nicky for a pet,

Steven wanted to learn

about green turtles.

He and his father went to the city.

They visited an aquarium.

The people there knew about animals
that live in the sea.

Steven told them about his turtle.

They said Nicky was a female.

They said few green turtles were left
in the sea.

Many had been killed by men.

They said it would be better

for Nicky to be free.

Nicky would go to a place

where there was turtle grass.

Turtle grass is a seaweed

that looks like long thin grass.

It grows in warm shallow water.

When Nicky got older,

she would mate with a male turtle.

She would come back to the beach

in Costa Rica to lay her eggs.

Baby turtles would hatch from them.

Steven and his father talked
about this on the way home.
They decided to let Nicky go.

Steven cried himself to sleep
that night.

Early in the morning he went

to Nicky's pen.

They played a game of tag.

Steven grabbed Nicky and hugged her.

That afternoon

Steven's father let Nicky go.

The turtle began to swim away.

Steven swam with her.

Nicky swam with her flippers.

Steven could not keep up with her.

He was sure he would never see

his pet again.

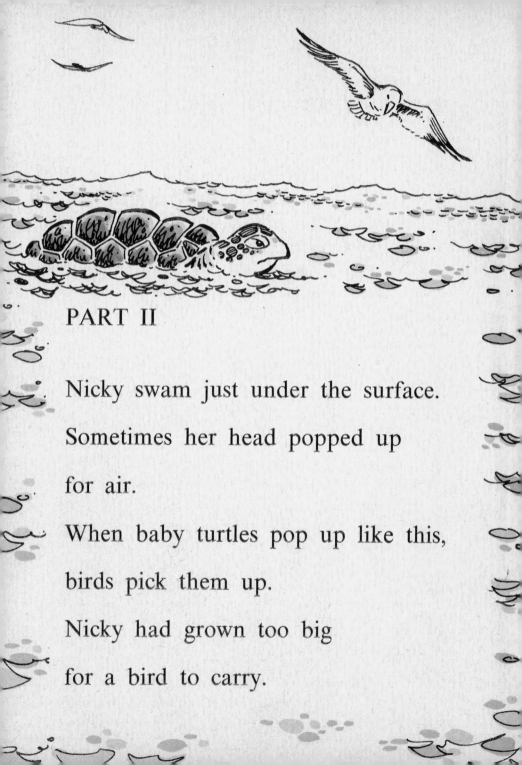

## PART II

Nicky swam just under the surface.

Sometimes her head popped up

for air.

When baby turtles pop up like this,

birds pick them up.

Nicky had grown too big

for a bird to carry.

But she was still not out of danger.

Large hungry fish lived in the sea.

One day Nicky saw two big shapes

in the water ahead.

They were sharks!

Nicky dived.

One of the sharks came after her.

She found a hole between some rocks.

The shark tried to poke its head

into the hole and grab Nicky.

But its head was too big.

The shark bit at the rocks.

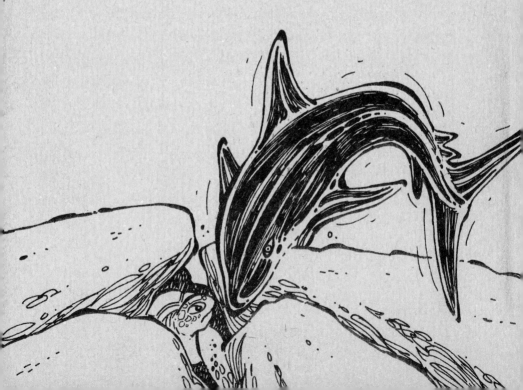

Nicky was safe as long as

she could hold her breath.

She could hold it for hours.

After a while the shark gave up

and swam away.

Later Nicky swam away too.

She rested on the bottom at night.

She swam during the day.

She swam for more than two weeks.

Then Nicky saw other green turtles.

She began to swim faster.

She came to a big field
of turtle grass.
After the long trip
Nicky was very hungry.
She ate and ate.

Then she found a rock underwater.

Nicky made this rock her home.

Every day she went to the field

of turtle grass.

Every night she went back to the rock.

Nicky got bigger and bigger.

When she was seven years old,

she weighed about one hundred pounds.

Her shell was big enough for

several children to sit on her back.

Steven was getting bigger too.

He often watched for Nicky.

When he was fourteen years old,

Steven began to help his uncle.

They caught fish

and green turtles for food.

# PART III

One day Nicky stopped

eating turtle grass.

She left her rock.

She started swimming back

to the place where she was born.

Now she was ready

to lay her eggs.

Other females started home too.

Some of them had been born

on the beach near Steven's house.

Somehow Nicky found her way.

She may have looked at the sun.

She may have felt

which way the water flowed

or how it smelled.

Maybe she tasted how salty it was.

Nicky could swim very fast.

And she was so big and hard

most fish could not eat her.

Even the sharks could not attack her.

But the turtle still had

one dangerous enemy. MAN!

Men tried to catch the green turtles

with nets and harpoons.

Off the beach, men waited

in boats.

Nicky came up for air near one boat.

A man saw her and raised a harpoon.

But there was someone else

in the boat.

It was Steven.

Steven was helping his uncle.

He saw the nicks

in the turtle's flippers.

"Stop!" Steven yelled.

He grabbed his uncle's arm.

"Don't kill that turtle," he said.

"I think it is Nicky."

"How can you be sure?"

his uncle asked.

"Have you ever seen another turtle

with nicks like that?" asked Steven.

His uncle said no.

"But we cannot be sure," he added.

"We must have meat to eat.
And we need money. We can sell
some of the meat and the shell."
Steven's uncle raised
his harpoon again.

"Don't," Steven pleaded.

"She is going to the beach
to lay eggs.
If you kill her now, there will be
no baby turtles."

Steven's uncle put down his harpoon.

"You are right," he said.

"I won't kill her."

Green turtles come

to the beach when it is dark.

That night Steven looked for Nicky.

But she did not come.

Every night Steven went to the beach.

One night the moon

was full and bright.

Steven saw a big turtle come

out of the water.

The turtle crossed the beach.

It began to dig a hole

with its back flippers.

Steven crept up behind the turtle.

He could see it clearly.

He looked at its front flippers.

There were nicks in the edges.

It was Nicky!

Steven was so happy he cried.

He hugged her.

Nicky finished digging the hole

and laid her eggs.

She covered her nest.

Then she started across the beach.

Steven rode to the sea on her back.

At the shore he said good-bye

to Nicky again.

"I'll see you when you come back

to lay more eggs," he said.

Steven dug up Nicky's eggs.

He buried them in his yard.

The next day he built a fence

around the nest.

This kept dogs from digging up

the eggs.

Steven waited two months.

Then he began to get up every day

before it was light.

He watched the nest.

At last a head popped

out of the sand.

Then all the babies came up

out of the sand.

There were about a hundred of them.

Steven saw one with nicks

in the edges of its flippers.

Steven picked it up.

"You look just like your momma,"

he said.

"I will call you Nicky Junior.

You can stay with me

while you are a baby.

I will keep you safe

from birds and crabs.

When your shell gets big and hard,

they will not be able to eat you.

Then I will let you go.

You can swim to the turtle grass

where your mother is.

She will come back to lay eggs again.

I will look for you both every year."